Fun with CORK

35 Do-It-Yourself Projects for Cork Accessories, Gifts, Decorations, and Much More!

JUTTA HANDRUP & MAIKE HEDDER

Translation: Andrea Jones Berasaluce

Skyhorse Publishing

CONTENTS

WHAT'S THIS BEAUTY?
COULD IT BE CORK?

That's what we thought in the summer of 2014 when we held the new cork materials in our hands for the first time. Before that, we, like many others probably, only knew of cork being used to make wine corks or bulletin boards and flooring.

This was no wine cork in front of us, rather fabrics and papers in many shapes and colors. At first, we couldn't believe these were really made of cork. The material instantly fascinated us. Cork delights your sense of touch: soft, light, and completely natural. At the same time, it's functional: easy to work with, water- and dirt-repellent, and versatile.

Many well-known crafting techniques lend themselves to cork, from the world of paper and fabric to adhesive film. All the cork formats thrilled us right away and we subjected them to our creative tests. We glued and checked it hourly if everything stuck fast, made marks on it with chocolate, marmalade, coffee, and red wine, experimented with water colors and acrylic paints, sewed, cut, punched holes, and hammered it. Cork's versatility surprised and persuaded us. In this book, we show you how to make DIY projects for beautiful decorations, small gift ideas, and accessories made of our new favorite material.

Let yourself catch our cork fever!

We wish you lots of fun crafting!
Jutta Handrup & Maike Hedder

CORK
AS **CRAFTING MATERIAL**

FEELS LOVELY

Cork is both wonderfully soft and smooth. It just feels pleasant and gives DIY projects a very special touch, in the purest sense of the word. Simply touch it and see for yourself!

NATURAL

Cork is a natural product, free from chemicals and synthetics. Therefore, children can play with your DIY projects or help make the crafts. If you want to forego animal products like leather, cork's a great substitute. We love small bags made of cork!

EASY TO WORK WITH

Cork is easy to cut and doesn't fray. Handling cork doesn't require learning new skills; you can simply apply your experience working with paper and fabric when crafting with cork.

WATER- AND DIRT-REPELLENT

Cork is water- and dirt-repellent, so you can put your DIY projects in the bathroom or kitchen without worrying. If, for example, a little food lands on your cork placemat, you can easily wipe it clean.

VERSATILE

Cork is available as paper, fabric, and adhesive film of various thicknesses. It doesn't just come in the pure cork design, but also in very unique patterns and colors. You can easily tailor all the projects in this book to suit your personal tastes.

CORK FABRIC

Cork fabric is firm, similar to leather, and easy to work with. The fabric is sold in different thicknesses and 2 substrates. In this book, we mainly work with thin cork fabric.

CORK ADHESIVE FILM

The adhesive film is thin and has a sticky surface on the back. It is very easy to cut and suitable for decorating an infinite number of objects.

APPEARANCE

- Comparable to soft leather
- Smooth, soft surface
- Top coated with cork pattern
- Underside is uniform shade of brown
- Thickness: just over 0.04 inches

- Top coated with cork
- Adhesive underside with removable protective film
- Thickness: very thin, less than 0.02 inches

CHARACTERISTICS

- Very tear-resistant
- Doesn't fray
- Doesn't bend/fold

- Adheres well to straight, smooth surfaces
- Stays on smooth walls, tiles, wood, plastic, porcelain (among others)
- Easily removed again
- Bends/folds

HANDLING

- Cutting
- Scoring
- Gluing
- Sewing
- Riveting
- Nailing
- Stapling
- Stamping
- Punching
- Painting
- Labeling

- Cutting
- Punching
- Stamping
- Tearing
- Gluing
- Painting
- Labeling

CORK **CONSTRUCTION PAPER**

Cork construction paper is very firm and coated on both sides with cork. You can use it similarly to normal construction paper, but it does have somewhat greater difficulty keeping its shape.

CORK **PAPER**

Cork paper is coated on 1 side and very thin. It works well for projects that call for thin paper such as origami or translucent crafts.

APPEARANCE

- Top and bottom coated with cork
- Thickness: 0.03 inches

- Surface coated with cork
- Underside is monochrome dark brown, paper substrate
- Thickness: 0.02 inches

CHARACTERISTICS

- Not tear-resistant
- Strong paper
- Less translucent
- Somewhat hard to bend/fold

- Not tear-resistant
- Bends/folds
- Translucent

HANDLING

- Cutting
- Gluing
- Creasing
- Punching
- Stamping
- Tearing
- Sewing
- Painting
- Labeling

- Cutting
- Tearing
- Punching
- Creasing
- Bending/Folding
- Stamping
- Gluing
- Sewing
- Painting
- Labeling

WHAT DO I NEED
TO MAKE CRAFTS USING CORK?

THE GOOD NEWS IS:
If you want to start crafting with cork right away, no need to go shopping first. Crafting fans will already have at least a few basics at home perfect for making crafts with cork.

YOU DON'T NEED ANY SPECIAL TOOLS.
Here we present for you a little preview of all the tools used in this book. Needless to say, in each project you'll also find a detailed description of the materials needed, along with tips.

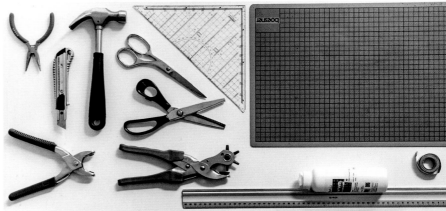

- Glue
- Punch and riveting pliers
- Hammer
- Paintbrush
- Scissors
- Cutting machine
- Cutter knife
- Novelty hole punches
- Hole punch
- Sewing machine
- Needle and thread
- Paper clips
- Compass
- Set squares
- Ruler
- Pens/markers
- Pliers

TIPS AND TRICKS
FOR CRAFTING WITH CORK

GLUING CORK

In principle, you can glue cork with ordinary superglue. However, we've had very good experiences using Rudolfix 333 rubber cement. When gluing 2 pieces of fabric, the gluing site doesn't completely harden right away and allows for flexible movement. The glue also sticks very quickly; an advantage for cork especially as it really wants to return to its original shape.

For best results, place a thin layer of glue on both surfaces you're gluing together and press them firmly together. After about 10 minutes, the glue should no longer slip, and after an hour, the bond should have set. When it comes to glued objects that will bear weight, make sure to let the adhesive surfaces dry and set for several hours. To this end, you can either use paper clips or bulldog clips, or weigh down the adhesive surfaces with several books.

SEWING CORK

Both cork fabric and cork paper lend themselves to sewing. With cork fabric, you can proceed similarly as you would when sewing a very firm fabric or leather. Our best experiences were with a special denim or leather needle. Nevertheless, make sure that you use a thick sewing machine needle. You need not serge the seams, as cork doesn't fray.

With cork paper, you should also take care to choose a longer stitch length to avoid perforating the cork.

CREASING, FOLDING, AND BENDING CORK

Cork paper adapts well to origami projects or other folding DIYs, even if cork paper is a bit harder to fold/bend than normal paper. It's best to fold the paper in both directions when creasing so that it forms a stronger bend, and then run a ruler or another hard object along the crease.

PAINTING CORK

Cork is generally water- and dirt-repellent. Thus, not all pens, markers, or paints are apt for coloring cork. You can use water colors to achieve beautiful background colors, though you should use somewhat less water than usual when mixing the paint. Acrylic paints keep well. As for the pens and markers you'd like to use for detailed drawings, patch test them first by cutting out a piece of any cork material of your choice and painting a few test stripes. We had very good experiences with most permanent markers.

For all colors, you should expect a slightly longer drying time before the colors become smudge-proof.

ACCESSORIES AND GIFTS

MADE OF CORK FABRIC

ROUND BRAIDED BRACELET

WE HAVE A FAVORITE BRACELET IN EVERY COLOR!

And why not? Learning to make round braids is easy and they're very quick to make once you master the technique. Combine with metallic end caps to create beautiful bracelets.

MATERIALS

- Glue
- 2 strips of cork fabric, thin (approx. 0.12"–0.1" wide and 31.5" long, in different colors if you like)
- Bracelet end caps

Tip

A lanyard can be a great help when braiding. Pull the knot through the key ring and hang the lanyard from a doorknob. That way the lanyard can keep the braiding good and tight.

HOW IT'S MADE

1. Lay the 2 strips over each other and pull them through a key ring (or a safety needle). Knot in the middle, so 4 equal-size cork strips hang down.

2. Take 2 strips from each side, cork pattern facing up. Now cross the strips once in the middle. Then, begin with the actual braiding.

1.

2.

3.

4.

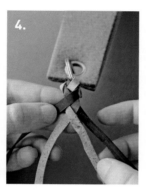

5.

6.

7.

8.

3. To do so, take the farthest left brown strip and, with a twist, lay it behind both middle strips. Then, with the cork side facing up, place it over and outside of the second strip from the right.

4. In the next step, bring the brown strip on the far right behind the middle 2 strips and place it over and outside of the second strip from the left, again with the cork side up. If working with strips in 2 different colors, you should now see a colored V in the middle.

5. Now, grab the purple strip on the far left and repeat Step 3. Then, with the purple strip on the far right, repeat step 4. Continue doing this until you reach the end of the bracelet.

6. Secure the end with a knot.

7. Measure your wrist, to know how long the cork strips should approximately be. Then, you can wrap the ends of the braided bracelet tightly with a nylon thread to prevent fraying. In the corresponding step photo, we used a white thread to bring out the visual. Follow this same process at the other end of the bracelet and cut the leftovers.

8. Put some glue in the end caps of the clasp. Stick 1 end of the bracelet into each cap.

ALTERNATIVE: 6-STRAND BRAID

The round braid also works with 6 strands. We braided the single-color bracelet in the photos using this method. To do it, take 3 strips of cork, knot them tightly and then, employing the same braiding method, bring the outer strips behind 3 strips and place them over and outside of the 3 strips on the other side.

STATEMENT BRACELET

....

THIS BRACELET MAKES A REAL STATEMENT

....

With beads and a glitter effect, this bracelet is a great eye-catcher for the evening!

MATERIALS

- Cork fabric, thin (3 strips, 0.08"–0.16" wide and approx. 9.8" long)
- Wide bracelet clasp (1.2")
- Various beads

TOOLS

- Glue
- Scissors
- Pliers

....
HOW IT'S MADE
....

1. First, start with a string about the length of your wrist. For best accuracy, briefly tape a string to the bracelet clasp to gauge the optimal length.

2. Then, cut 3 cork strips, approx. 0.12"–0.20" wide and at the length you measured. Cut a nylon thread for the beads with an additional 1.2" of length.

3. Knot the end several times and thread the beads, until reaching your desired bracelet length. You must also knot the end multiple times so the small circular knots stay in place.

4. Push the strips into the clasp in the order you desire and close it with the pliers. With the second clasp, make sure you keep this same order.

NOTE ON THE MATERIALS

You can find bracelet clasps and beads at well-stocked craft stores with a jewelry selection or online.

The statement bracelet is particularly pretty if you combine a set of slightly different colored small beads with some larger eye-catching beads.

CUDDLY COFFEE MUG HOLDER

WE PREFER TO DRINK OUR COFFEE HOT!

To not burn our fingers, we created this sweet coffee cup holder.

MATERIALS

- Cork fabric (approx. 5.9" × 15.7")
- Approx. 15.7" felting wool yarn

TOOLS

- Scissors
- Hole punch

HOW IT'S MADE

1. Cut out a cork strip sized to adequately fit around your coffee mug. Punch evenly-spaced holes along the edge and thread your felting wool yarn through them. Knot the ends and you're done!

2. Determine the shape of the strip needed based on the cup.

3. If your mug widens at the top, give your cork strip a gentle curved shape, so it fits well. You can best determine the perfect shape for your mug using a test pattern made of paper. Glue 2 A4-size pieces of paper back-to-back and lay them on the table. Draw a ring around the mug at your preferred height, using well-diluted water color paint.

4. Lay the mug on the paper and roll it once over the sheets. You now have a mark on the paper, which you can cut out and use like a stencil.

CLUTCH

SINCE CORK FABRIC DOESN'T FRAY, IT'S IDEAL FOR SIMPLE SEWING PROJECTS.

....

Combine 2 different fabrics together to sew yourself a unique clutch in 15 minutes. You can also thread a ribbon through the sides and use it as a shoulder bag.

....
HOW IT'S MADE
....

The clutch consists of 2 parts, a back and a front. The back of the clutch is somewhat longer, as it also doubles as the flap, which you then fold forward. After you just sew the back and the front together.

1. Cut 2 pieces of cork for the front and back sides, as seen in the sketch.

2. Now, sew the front side onto the bottom of the back side. Set the 2 pieces of fabric exactly on top of each other, with the pretty outsides facing each other, and pin them into place.

3. Using the sewing machine, sew the 2 pieces of fabric on both sides of the edges and the bottom.

4. Turn the bag inside out.

MATERIALS
- 2 pieces of cork fabric

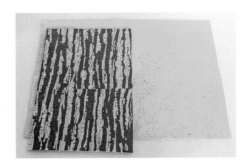

Back: 11" wide, 12.2" long
Front: 11" wide, 7.1" long
See Sketch

TOOLS
- Scissors
- Sewing Machine
- Pins
- Ruler

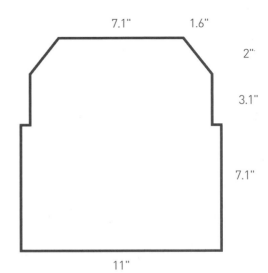

ACCESSORIES AND GIFTS MADE OF CORK FABRIC

Tip

Vary the bags by using different cork patterns and straps or decorate them using a black permanent marker.

SMARTPHONE CASE (NO SEWING!)

....

THE GREAT THING ABOUT THIS SMARTPHONE CASE IS:

....

You don't need to be able to sew at all and once you get the hang of it, you can also make a tablet case or glue a protective sleeve onto your laptop.

MATERIAL SPECS

For a smartphone, an A4-sized piece of cork fabric will do. Thin fabric works better for gluing.

MATERIALS

- Cork fabric
- Suede strap

TOOLS

- Rubber cement
- Paper clips
- Scissors
- Ruler
- Cutter knife

HOW IT'S MADE
....

The cell phone case has a front and a back. The back side and the foldable flap consist of 1 piece of cork fabric.

1. Measure the width and length of your smartphone and leave an extra 0.4" as an adhesive surface. The adhesive surfaces are located on the bottom as well as on both sides of the front and back of the case. There are 6 adhesive surfaces in total. Outline the front and back sides on the cork.

2. Now, cut out 2 pieces of fabric and fold the adhesive surfaces inward, so you can glue them more easily.

3. Lay the front side onto the back, with the pretty cork surface facing outward. The front's adhesive surfaces should therefore be on the outside, while the back's adhesive surfaces are on the inside. First, glue the 2 lower adhesive surfaces and press them firmly together. Fix the gluing sites in place with a paper clip and let them dry for an hour.

4. Then, glue the 2 side pieces, one right after the other, and let the sides dry while pressed firmly together for at least an hour.

5. The case is now almost finished. Cut a strap long enough to wrap around the case twice and knot it.

6. Using the cutter knife, make 2 little slits near the top of the back of the case. Thread the strap through them and knot it tightly on the inside. To shut the case, stick the flap under the suede strap.

WAIST BELT WITH STARS

....

DON'T HAVE A BELT FOR YOUR NEW DRESS?

....

You can very easily fashion a one-of-a-kind belt from cork fabric, without needing a sewing machine. With a novelty hole punch, you can decorate a most beautiful belt.

MATERIALS

- Cork fabric
- Snap fasteners

TOOLS

- Novelty hole punch (star shape)
- Scissors
- Ruler
- Rubber cement
- Needle and thread
- Tape measure

MATERIAL SPECS

Length varies based on person, approx. 1.2"–2" × 27.6"–35.4". It's best to use the thin fabric, as it's the most suited to gluing and punching.

HOW IT'S MADE

....

1.
Determine your preferred belt width and length using a tape measure and cut out the corresponding fabric strips.

2.
Now, punch evenly-spaced stars into the fabric. Repeat on the opposite side of the fabric strip.

3.
Turn the belt over and determine where to place the snap fasteners on the front. Tightly sew by hand both parts of the snap fastener into their corresponding locations on the belt.

4.
Glue a punched-out star onto the visible top of the snap fastener.

5.
Cut out a small beltloop. The fabric strip should be somewhat longer than the width of the belt, so it can be glued on. Glue the beltloop on tightly, so the belt just fits exactly through and doesn't sit loosely.

6.
Set the gluing sites in place with a paper clip and let dry and harden for at least 3 hours.

Tip

Switch up the various cork fabrics and the belts' widths. That way you'll always have a fitting accessory for different outfits.

NOTEBOOKS

····················
**YOU CAN NEVER HAVE
ENOUGH NOTEBOOKS!**
····················

We make these little everyday compa-
nions ourselves in the colors and sizes
we like. For a classic look, combine
pure cork fabric with white paper. If
you're after something more colorful,
combine different materials and paper
colors to your heart's delight.

MATERIALS

- Paper or colored paper
- Cork fabric or cork construction paper
  (A4, or whatever size you like)
- Undyed yarn

TOOLS

- Sewing machine
- Cutting machine or scissors
- Set squares or ruler
- Cutter knife

HOW IT'S MADE

1. You can sew any size notebook. First, cut the paper for the notebook pages in your desired size. These will later be folded in the middle; so, 1 piece of paper will serve as 2 notebook pages. Of course, you can also just use A5 paper in landscape format. When cutting the pages, it's best to use the set squares and cutting machine to make even pages.

2. Carefully fold the sheets in the middle. If using firmer paper, run a ruler over the fold to create a neat crease. With very firm paper, first draw the ruler along the desired fold location. Then, lay the ruler near the desired fold and fold it once over the line using a pointed object.

3. Place all the pages together, like in a book. If working with firm paper, the middle pages will protrude a bit. Shorten the protruding pieces with a cutting machine or a cutter knife.

4. Cut a rectangle of cork fabric. It should be somewhat larger than the unfolded pages. If using paper smaller than A5, go approx. 0.2" wider than the page, and for larger sizes, approx. 0.4". Anticipate the more space you have, the more pages you can have. Position the paper in the middle of the cork fabric. The cork side should face

down. With the sewing machine, stitch once exactly over the pages' crease. Briefly stitch back and forth at the beginning and end.

5. For the closure, cut a cork strip; approx. 0.2"–0.4" wide and 4 times as long as the closed notebook. Use the cutter knife to make a small slit in the fabric on the front of the notebook. Mind that you don't cut into the pages. The cork strip should just fit through the slit. Pull the strip through the slit and knot the end. Now, you can close your notebook with the strap. Adjust the length to your liking.

Tip

- You can use a pair of scissors instead of a cutting machine.

- You can also use cork construction paper to make a case for your notebook!

- Collect extra pretty magazine pages or paper to later incorporate as notebook paper.

TASSELS OR KEYCHAINS

....

LOOKING FOR A CUTE LITTLE GIFT FOR YOUR FRIEND?

....

How about a homemade tassel? You can wear it as jewelry or put it on a key ring or hang it from a handbag. Add a few pendants or charms to make it a very personal adornment.

MATERIALS

- Cork fabric, thin (for size, see note)
- End cap
- Glue
- In addition (optional): charms, chains, and jewelry pendants

HOW IT'S MADE

1. Cut a piece of fabric to the size you want. For this project, we work with a 3.1" × 2.6" piece, suitable for an end cap 0.3" across. Slit the fabric at regular intervals. Always stop approx. 0.8" from the end, meaning your slits are just 2.4" of the 3.1". **You can prepare charms or pendants, hanging them from jewelry chains with the help of split jewelry rings.**

2. Wind the piece of fabric as tightly as possible and test if the top fits into the end cap. It should just fit inside. The pendants or chains are wrapped in during the last twist, just before the end.

3. Then, brush a thin layer of glue onto the fabric on the back of the non-fringed surface, thinly roll up the fabric, and press it firmly. Take care in doing this so that the ends of the pendant chains hang only in the lower third of the end piece. Let dry for at least 10 minutes. After that, the glued part should shorten enough that it disappears almost entirely into the cap.

4. Dab glue onto the end and push the tassel into the end cap. Let dry for at least 24 hours before using.

ACCESSORIES AND GIFTS MADE OF CORK FABRIC

You can find great sayings for fortune cookies everywhere:

The fortune cookies make an extra special impression if you mix in a few funny anecdotes or personalized messages. Simply use familiar place names or other similar things from your surroundings!

FORTUNE COOKIES

WE LIKE TO GIVE A LITTLE LUCK NOW AND THEN!

Everyone likes a nice message in a fortune cookie. Future predictions are a guaranteed hit at your next New Year's Eve party and they'll give the guests will a nice conversation topic. This type of cookie can always be refilled with new messages.

MATERIALS

- Cork fabric (for a small fortune cookie, you'll need a circle 3.1" across)
- Thread
- Small pieces of notepaper for secret messages
- A small piece of glitter sticker paper

TOOLS/AUXILIARY MATERIALS

- Round stencil (circle/compass or coffee cup, saucer, etc.)
- Sewing Machine
- Ruler

HOW IT'S MADE

1. Using the stencil, draw a round circle on the cork fabric. For a small fortune cookie, the diameter should run 3.1"–3.5". Cut out the circle with a pair of pinking shears.

2. Fold the circle once in the middle, so the cork side is on the inside. Lay the half circle in front of you so the straight side is toward you. Now, using the sewing machine, sew a small seam perpendicular to the straight side, right in the middle, slightly offset from the fold (see photo). Take care not to make the seam too long, and sew it back and forth, so the seam remains fixed.

3. Now, fold the fabric once on both sides of the seam. This creates the typical fortune cookie shape. Write a small message and put it inside the cookie. To make it particularly eye-catching, we cut out small hearts from the glitter paper and pasted them on the message.

CORK FABRIC DECORATIONS

FLOWERPOT HANGER

HANG THE MOST BEAUTIFUL
FLOWERS IN YOUR FIELD OF SIGHT.

With a bit of cork fabric and a
pretty flowerpot, you can create
a completely personalized
flowerpot hanger and transform
your balcony or garden into an
oasis of well-being.

Have a vintage bowl? Make it into
a hanging fruit bowl in the kitchen.

MATERIALS

- Cork fabric, thin
- Flowerpot
- Thin rope

TOOLS

- Hole punch
- Hammer
- Ruler
- Scissors (or cutting machine if available)
- Tubular rivets

MATERIAL SPECS

- 3 strips **for the base**, 1" × 15.8"
- 3 strips **for the handle**, 0.6" × 11.8"

1.

The length of the fabric strips can vary based on the shape of the bowl or flowerpot. For a flowerpot 5.9" tall and 7.1" across, we used 1" × 15.7" fabric strips for the base. If in doubt, you can always start with a longer strip and shorten it.

2.

Now, with the hole punch, make a small hole at both ends of the fabric strips as well as in the middle.

3.

Lay the 3 cork strips together in a star shape. The middles should be on top of each other. Push a tubular rivet through all 3 holes in the center and place the other half of the rivet right on top. (See Figure 1.)

4.

Take care not to change the position of the cork strips and then hammer the rivet into place.

5.

Now, you need the loop handles. Cut out 3 fabric strips and, using the hole punch, make holes at both ends of each.

6.

Fit the handles together with the thicker fabric strips. Place the flowerpot exactly in the center of the star-shaped cork strips. (See Figure 2.)

7.

Cross the ends of every 2 wide cork strips laying near each other. (See Figure 3.)

8.

Attach these 2 cork strips with a thin loop handle. The loop should face upward. (See Figure 4.) Fasten the 2 fabric strips and loop together with a rivet. Repeat this process with the other fabric strips.

9.

Now, place the bowl/flowerpot in the middle of the cork structure. Draw a thin rope through the handle and hang up the flower hanger.

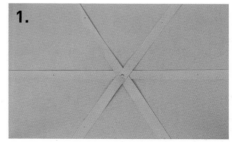

Tip

Practice sewing with the sewing machine and cork fabric beforehand, on leftover fabric, in order to optimally calibrate your machine.

CUSHIONS WITH FEATHERS

. . . .

SINGLE-COLOR CUSHIONS CAN BE MADE BEAUTIFULLY UNIQUE.

. . . .

We prettified a pillow with an ombre gradient.

MATERIALS	TOOLS	MATERIAL SPECS

MATERIALS

- Cork fabric
- Cushion cover
- Cushion
- Stencil

TOOLS

- Pencil
- Scissors
- Pins
- Sewing machine and thread

MATERIAL SPECS

For each feather, a piece of A4-sized fabric.

HOW IT'S MADE

1.
Print and cut out feather stencils or other stencil shapes of choice and transfer the shape to the fabric. You can also draw the feathers freehand on the back of the fabric.

2.
Cut out the shapes with scissors.

3.
Position the 2 feathers on the cushion cover and stick them into place by putting pins along the sides.

4.
Using the sewing machine, sew, with a straight stitch, once lengthwise through the middle of the feather from the tip to the quill.

Repeat this with the second feather.

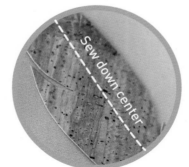

Sew down center

PLACEMATS

Due to its liquid-repellent surface, cork fabric is ideal for coasters, placemats, chargers, etc.

MATERIALS

- Cork fabric   • Stencil

TOOLS

- Scissors or a cutter knife   • Cutting mat/surface

MATERIAL SPECS

- A3 size per set

All cork fabrics are suitable.

HOW IT'S MADE

1.
Print and cut out the stencils and transfer the shape to the fabric. You can also draw the shape free-hand on the back of the fabric.

2.
Cut out the stencil pieces and transfer them to the fabric.

3.
Now, you just have to cut out the fabric pieces and the place-mat's finished!

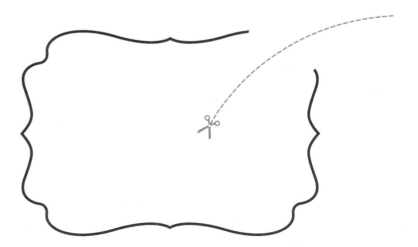

Tip

If you want to design your own shape, you should first measure the required size for the stencil using your plates. Then, either draw the borders on the back of the fabric or create your own shapes with an image editor, which you can then print out as your stencil.

STAR ORNAMENT WITH DECORATIVE THREAD

Small star ornaments made of cork are quick to sew and look just as good on branches as hanging in a window.

For extra flair, we have taken colored thread and sewn it on in loose layers—dark blue or pink thread goes particularly well with cork fabric.

HOW IT'S MADE

1.
Cut out a star stencil in whatever size you like.

2.
Then, prepare a corresponding rectangle of cork fabric. The star should fit twice within the rectangle.

3.
Fold it together with the cork facing outward and transfer the star onto 1 of the 2 sides.

4.
Now, stitch once over the star's outline using the sewing machine. Leave a small part open and stuff the star with a little cotton.

This works best if you use a pen or a knitting needle to push the cotton into the corners.

5.
Use the sewing machine to stitch several times along the star in loose layers. To do so, stitch once along the line and then loosely next to it.

Finish on a star point and leave about 7.9" of thread. This will later serve to hang up the ornament.

6.
Lastly, carefully cut the star out.

MATERIALS

- Any number of rectangular pieces of cork fabric (approx. 3.9" × 7.9" per star)
- Star stencil
- Erasable fabric pen
- Some cotton
- Colorful sewing thread

TOOLS

- Sewing machine
- Scissors

Tip

The star is cut out in the last step, which makes it easier for you to get the hang of sewing the fabric!

With an erasable fabric pen, you can trace the star's outline on the cork fabric. The marks disappear after a few hours or days.

HEART-SHAPED PICTURE COLLAGE

DON'T LET YOUR LOVELY PICTURES COLLECT DUST.

Don't leave your lovely pictures or favorite postcards in a box to collect dust. Create a beautiful mural with them instead!

The handy thing about this photo collage is: you can always easily switch out the photos or postcards.

HOW IT'S MADE

1. Consider from the beginning how large the heart should be. That depends, naturally, on how many photos you want to place on it. So, sort your photos first and lay them on the fabric to determine the size. The size of the heart in the example is 28.7" × 23.6".

2. Draw the heart on the back of the fabric with a pencil and cut it out.

3. Turn the heart so the pretty side faces upward and place it on a cutting surface. Then, arrange the photos on the front side of the fabric heart.

4. Using the cutter knife, make a small slit in the fabric, approx. 0.6" long, under each of the 4 corners of every photo. Stick the corners of the photos through these slits.

5. Now, hang the heart on the wall. Use adhesive picture hangers, nailed firmly or stuck on with wide double-sided tape if hanging it on a door.

MATERIALS

- Cork fabric
- Adhesive mounting hooks
- Double-sided tape
- Nails

TOOLS

- Cutter knife
- Cutting mat/surface
- Pencil
- Scissors

Tip

The pure black-and-white collage appears very chic and minimal. This effect can also be achieved with color pictures. When choosing, look for a consistent color scheme.

Also think about the color combination of the pictures with the cork and keep in mind that you can buy the fabric in different colors.

LOVE VASES OR LANTERNS

OUR SET OF LOVE GLASSES EXUDES TONS OF LOVE.

Naturally you can make these vases or lanterns spell any word—how about your name?

The glasses are quite versatile and can serve as vases for small bouquets or as lanterns.

MATERIALS

- 4 glasses
- Cork fabric
- Eyelets (0.16," about 50)

TOOLS

- Hole punch
- Rivet pliers
- Erasable fabric pen (if available)
- Glue

HOW IT'S MADE

Measure the height and circumference of the glasses and cut 4 corresponding rectangles of cork fabric. The height should match the height of the glasses. For the length, add 0.4"–0.6" to the circumference.

You can sketch the letters by hand or use this little trick:

In order for the letters on the glasses to be about the same size, it's best if you cut a small paper rectangle as an aid.

You can position this on the back of the cork fabric. Measure the distance between the paper's edge and the fabric's edge and make sure it's the same for all the glasses. Mark the 4 corners on the back of the fabric using the erasable fabric pen. For the letters L, V, and E, use the corners and endpoints for the letters' lines. Remember to draw the L and E back-to-front. For the O, place the highest and the lowest point on the edges of the paper.

Using the hole punch, make holes in the fabric—you may have to roll it up tightly. Begin at the corners and then make holes evenly in between. To finish, put an eyelet in each hole, place the strips on the glasses, and glue the overhanging ends.

WHITE DESIGNER TABLE

Cork not only goes great in nature-themed establishments with a lot of wood; combining it with metal, smooth surfaces, concrete, a white tabletop, and designer furniture gives cork a stylish touch.

MATERIALS

- Glue
- Cork fabric
- End table (Model shown from IKEA)

TOOLS

- Scissors
- Pencil

MATERIAL SPECS

22" × 22" in this example but the amount of material depends on the size of your table.

Within just minutes, a white lacquered metal table becomes a unique designer piece for the home.

HOW IT'S MADE

1. Measure the table's surface and transfer the dimensions to the cork fabric.

2. Cut the cork fabric and glue the back tightly onto the table's surface.

Tip

The simple cork fabric color will also go well with silver-colored metal and gray or blue shades.

CORK UPGRADES
FOR WALLS

AND **ADHESIVE CORK DECORATIONS**

GEOMETRIC BUTTERFLY

We're big fans of masking tape, with which you can quickly conjure up ideas for decorations that are easy to remove again.

Cork masking tape is our newest passion. A hip geometric butterfly now adorns our kitchen wall. Of course, you can also stick other abstract shapes onto the wall!

MATERIALS

- Adhesive cork

TOOLS

- Set squares
- Scissors (or, if available, cutting machine)
- Pencil
- Ruler

MATERIAL SPECS

25 strips:
0.6" wide, lengths shown in sketch:

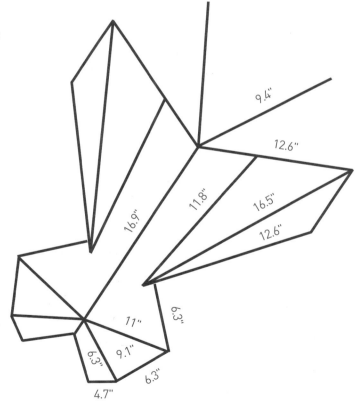

For a clean look, it's important to have no gaps between cutting sites. Glue the strips slightly overlapping each other.

If you want a 100 percent symmetrical picture, you can sketch the shape onto the wall in pencil beforehand.

You can cut straight strips more easily with the cutting machine rather than scissors. Fold the adhesive film once in the middle and, with the cutting machine, cut so the strips are doubly long. The fold should disappear by itself from the film after you stick it onto a surface.

It's best to stick the film onto a smooth, straight wall and not on one with wallpaper.

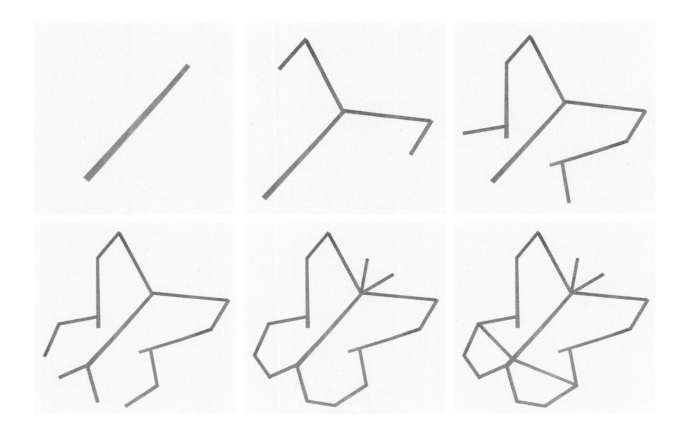

1.

Whether you want to stick on a butterfly or your own design, it's best to draw a small sketch first as a guide.

2.

Using the cutting machine, cut 25 strips of the adhesive film. Now shorten a few strips in accordance with the sketch and sort the strips according to their position. If you notice when sticking on a strip that you have cut it too short, you can simply stick another piece over it. As seen in the pattern, no gap should stand out between any 2 strips.

3.

The simple cork fabric color will also go well with silver colored metal and gray or blue shades. Begin sticking the strips on with the middle part. This determines the butterfly's approximate position on the wall.

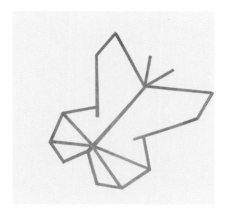

4.
It's easiest if you stick 1 strip on the right or left wing and then stick on the corresponding strip on the other side. Then, keep working bit by bit. Mark some small auxiliary lines in pencil.

5.
First stick on the butterfly's external shape and, afterward, the inner strips. If you want to correct something, the adhesive strips can be easily lifted again and pulled off the wall without a hitch. Overhanging parts you can carefully cut away at the end by using a cutter knife directly on the wall.

SCRAPBOOKING, LABELS, AND CORK CONFETTI

YOU CAN MAKE GREAT THINGS EVEN FROM THE SMALLEST LEFTOVER ADHESIVE CORK SNIPPETS.

With our novelty hole punches, we craft labels super quickly. We love quick round cork labels; just punch one out and you're done. These not only look good on marmalade jars, but also enhance scrapbooking projects.

And from the very smallest odds and ends, using a normal hole punch, we make confetti!

MATERIALS

- Scrap pieces of adhesive cork
- Novelty or normal hole punches

HOW IT'S MADE

We don't leave any of our leftover pieces in a drawer, working directly with them instead. Simply punch your desired shapes out of the adhesive film. That way you'll always have a small stock of labels/stickers ready for DIY projects or gift packages.

Stationery shops conveniently sell sets of blank white cards. We always have a stack at home. Alternatively, you can use a cutting machine to cut the cards out yourself from white construction paper. If you do so, be sure that the cards will fit into a standard envelope to avoid unnecessary higher postage fees.

Black construction paper can also serve as a very classy base for cards!

GREETING CARDS

....

WE LOVE HANDWRITTEN MAIL!

....

It's even nicer if the card itself is also handmade. With some adhesive cork, you can conjure up endless types of beautiful cards. Let's show you our favorites!

MATERIALS

- Blank cards
- Adhesive cork (1 A4-sized piece for all cards)
- Pen (thinner fineliner)

TOOLS

- Cutter knife
- Cutting mat/surface
- Scissors

....

HOW IT'S MADE

....

PENNANT CHAIN CARDS

To make a pennant chain card, cut out small rectangles from the adhesive cork, then remove a small triangle from the lower edge. This creates a small pennant. Draw a line in pen across the card and hang your pennants from it.

CHRISTMAS TREE

Cut out triangles in different sizes from the adhesive film and arrange them into a Christmas tree on the card.

TEXT CARDS

For cards with lettering, you can easily look for a font you like in Microsoft Word or another word processing program. Type the word you want, enlarge the text, select it, and try out different fonts until you find one that appeals to you. Print out the letters on paper. Lay the paper onto the adhesive cork and set it in place with some tape. Cut out the letters with the cutter knife, then stick them onto the card.

WALL LETTERING

....

YOUR FAVORITE MOTTO ON THE WALL.

....

Your favorite motto in the hallway or above the sofa, a motivational saying in the study, or your wedding date in the bedroom—there are an endless number of ideas for beautiful messages on your walls and doors.

If you get bored and it's time for a fresh motto, just pull it off and craft yourself a new one. The adhesive film sticks well to smooth walls without wallpaper and can be removed again easily and without leaving marks.

MATERIAL

- Adhesive cork
- Printer paper

TOOLS

- Scissors
- Pencil
- Microsoft Word or other word processing program
- Printer

MATERIAL SPECS

- Custom sizing, (4.7" × 55.1" in the example shown)

HOW IT'S MADE

....

1. Test out different fonts for your lettering on the computer in Microsoft Word or other word processing program. The individual letters should be wide enough that you can easily cut them out along their outlines.

2. Adjust the font size until you are happy. In our example, about 4 letters fit on A4 paper in landscape format. Then, you can print and cut out the stencils.

3. Cut a long, straight strip of adhesive cork, onto which you can transfer your lettering.

4. First, on the back of the film, draw a horizontal line just straight under the lettering. Arrange the cut-out letters back-to-front on it.

5. Now, you can transfer the letters onto the back with the help of a stencil. If you've chosen a flowing font, the small connections between the letters can get lost when printing out the stencil, so add these again.

6. When you are content, carefully cut out the entire text and stick it onto the surface of your choice.

Tip

Note that even if curved and thin letters look good, they're much harder to cut out than thick, straight letters.

LETTER MUGS

. . . .

GIVE YOUR TOOTHBRUSHES AN ELEGANT HOME!

. . . .

Glamorize and personalize your toothbrush mug with your own initials.
Then, you can find your own toothbrush, even with tired eyes.

MATERIALS

- Adhesive cork (max. 3.9" × 3.9" per letter)
- White mug
- Paper

TOOLS

- Cutter knife
- Cutting mat/surface
- Microsoft Word or other word processing program
- Printer
- Tape

HOW IT'S MADE

. . . .

1. Measure the mug and determine the size of the letter(s) you'll be using. The mugs in the example shown are 2.4" tall.

2. Using Microsoft Word or another word processing program, choose a font that's thick enough to cut out the letter(s) when printed. Set the font size to fit the size of the mug you'll be using. In the example shown of the approx. 2.4" tall letter, we chose a font size of about 150 points in the "Baskerville" font.

3. Print out the desired letter(s) on a sheet of paper.

4. Place the adhesive film with adhesive facing downward (cork facing upward) onto the cutting surface and lay the paper on top. Tape the paper into place.

5. Carefully cut out the letters using the cutter knife. This way you're cutting through the paper and the adhesive film underneath it. Make sure that the paper doesn't move.

6. Once you've cut out the letters, stick them onto the mug.

CORK UPGRADES FOR WALLS AND ADHESIVE CORK DECORATIONS

DRAWER DECORATIONS

Mark your territory at home with your own initials or the abbreviations of your choice.

MATERIALS

- Adhesive cork (max. 3.9" × 3.9" per letter)
- Paper

TOOLS

- Cutter knife
- Cutting mat/surface
- Microsoft Word or other word processing program
- Printer
- Tape

HOW IT'S MADE

1. Measure each drawer and determine the size of the letter(s) you'll be using.

2. Using Microsoft Word or another word processing program, choose a font that's thick enough to cut out the letter(s) when printed. Set the font size to fit the size of the mug you'll be using.

3. Print out the desired letter(s) on a sheet of paper.

4. Place the adhesive film with adhesive facing downward (cork facing upward) onto the cutting surface and lay the paper on top. Tape the paper into place.

5. Carefully cut out the letters using the cutter knife. This way you're cutting through the paper and the adhesive film underneath it. Make sure that the paper doesn't move.

6. Once you've cut out the letters, stick them onto the drawers.

FOLD · CUT · GLUE

CORK PAPER BEAUTIES

ENVELOPES

CORK JUST FEELS GORGEOUS.

....

If you use cork as an envelope, your mail will make a great impression the very first time you place it in the mailbox. Inside, a colorful surprise awaits the recipient.

MATERIALS

- Cork paper (A4)
- Printer paper
- Standard envelope

TOOLS

- Watercolors
- Paintbrush
- Glue

....

HOW IT'S MADE

....

1. First, make a template for your envelopes by holding a standard envelope over hot water. The glued points should loosen so that you can pull them apart and use it as a template.

2. For the inner part of the envelope, paint a sheet of printer paper using watercolors. Use a combination of 3 to 4 colors and paint away. It's nice if you can see the brush strokes. Don't use too much water, so the paper won't buckle. Let it dry thoroughly.

3. Transfer your stencil once onto the cork paper and once onto the painted paper. Cut away 0.04" to 0.08" along the edges of the painted paper.

4. Assemble the cork envelope by folding normally, but fold the painted paper the other way around.

5. Glue both envelopes and insert the paper envelope inside the cork envelope. Glue it firmly into place.

Post für Dich

MINI ORIGAMI STARS FOR A MOBILE

....

CORK AND BIRCHWOOD GO JUST PERFECTLY TOGETHER.

....

With a little patience, from 2 materials you can create one lovely star mobile for the wall. Twinkle, twinkle, little star!

MATERIALS

- Approx. 40 strips of cork paper (1" × 17.3")
- Dried birch branch
- Transparent nylon thread
- Golden lacquer spray

TOOLS

- Needle
- Scissors

FOLDING STARS

1. First make a loop at the end of the paper strip. Be sure when doing so that the back side of the paper faces you (Figure 1).

2. Carefully place the end of the paper strip through the loop and pull it tight, then press everything flat. Before you should now be a pentagon (Figure 2). Fold the protruding end onto the pentagon.

3. Wrap the paper strip carefully around the pentagon (Figure 3). Always make sure that the corners lay neatly on top of each other (Figure 4).

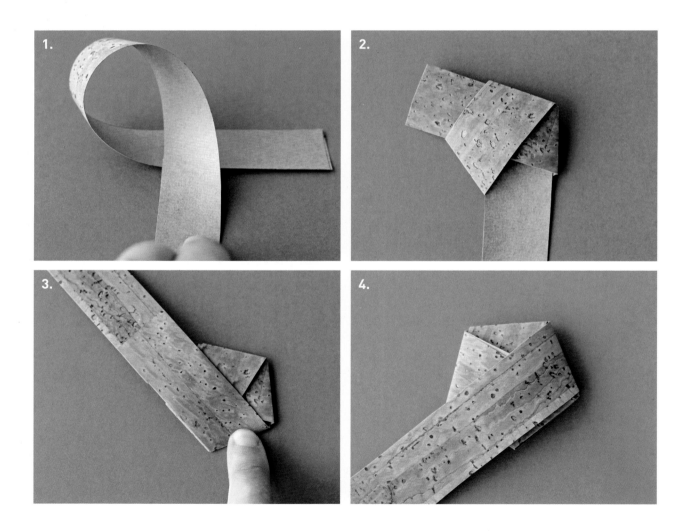

4. When you reach the end (Figure 5), stick the last part of the strip carefully under the previous layer (Figure 6).

5. Now, press all 5 sides down carefully with your fingernails or a ruler so that the star shape keeps (Figure 7).

HANGING AND SO FORTH

As an extra eye-catcher, we sprayed the star with golden lacquer. Let it dry well. Then, use a needle and thread to thread approximately 5 to 6 stars along the same thread. Vary the lengths a bit to create a nice effect. Hang the chains on the branch.

You can wrap the ends of the branch itself with thick yarn and then hang it from a nail.

HAND LETTERING ART

....

EVERYONE'S EXCITED ABOUT THE HAND LETTERING TREND!

....

The fever will soon grip those who haven't caught it yet. Just snatch up your favorite pen and practice drawing different fonts and compositions during free time or in the evenings on the sofa.

MATERIALS

- 2 sheets of cork paper
- Picture frames

TOOLS

- Scissors
- Practice/scrap paper
- Black permanent marker

HOW IT'S MADE

1. First cut the cork paper so it will fit into your picture frame.
2. Using permanent marker on cork paper, design your composition consisting of sayings and drawings, then frame the work.

Tips

HAND LETTERING

Before you start, of course, you have to look for inspiration. Do you have a favorite motto that you want to immortalize?

Once you've chosen a saying, consider in which font you'd like to draw the words by trying out the different fonts on your computer as inspiration.

Practice the letter composition on a bit on scrap paper until you are satisfied. Lastly, consider how you can decorate the text with small drawings.

GIFT BOXES

A BEAUTIFUL GIFT PACKAGE MAKES GIVING PRESENTS DOUBLY FUN.

These gift boxes are suited for small, thoughtful tokens. The advantage to cork paper:
It is moisture-repellent so it can also hold small beauty gifts like bath bombs or lotion bars!

MATERIALS

- 2 square pieces of cork paper

TOOLS

- Scissors
- Ruler
- Set squares

NOTE ON THE MATERIALS

The neutral cork paper box in the photo shown here was folded from a square with 9.8" sides, resulting in a box 3.1" to 3.5" wide.

The lid's side length should be 0.4" (for small boxes) to 0.8" (for larger boxes).

1. Cut 2 squares of cork paper in whatever size you want. Use the ruler and set squares to get perfect squares. The bottom and lid will be folded exactly the same way. Repeat this process with the smaller square and you can easily push the 2 halves gently into each other.

2. Fold the paper once vertically in the middle (Figure 2).

3. Unfold the sheet again and fold it anew horizontally (Figure 3).

4. After that, fold it once more diagonally (Figure 4).

5. You should now see a square with star-shaped folding lines before you (Figure 5).

6. Fold each corner to the middle junction point (Figure 6), so there is a smaller square in front of you.

7. Lay it right in front of you and fold the top and bottom sides into the middle (Figure 7).

8. Fold the folded sides again. Then, fold the top and bottom points again, so the sheets remain folded (Figure 8).

9. Then, fold the 2 side pieces into the middle (Figure 9).

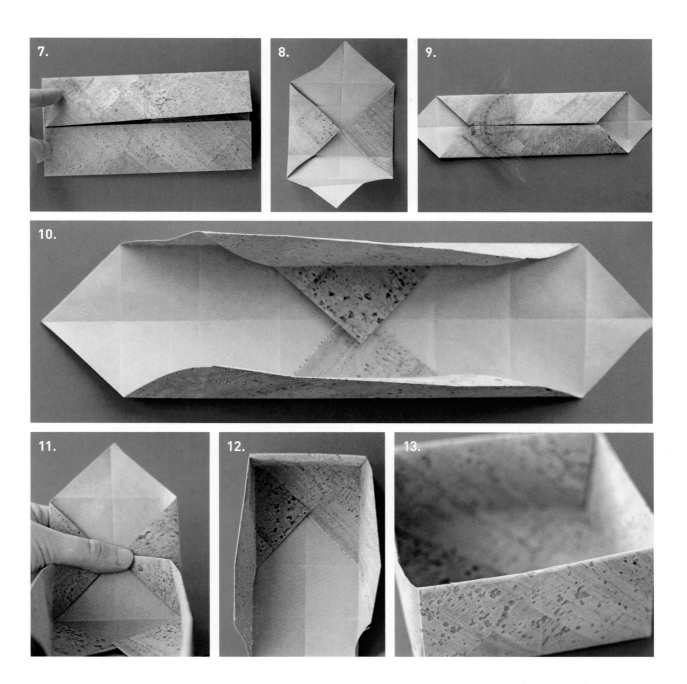

10. Do not quite fold all the way. Instead, leave it standing at a 90-degree angle (Figure 10).

11. Now, take the upper point and fold it in. In doing so, press the side walls lightly so that the upper side wall stands up, then press the point into the bottom (Figures 11 and 12).

12. Repeat step 11 on the lower side to create a finished half-box (Figure 13). Repeat all the steps and you'll have 2 halves, which you can stick together!

MORAVIAN STAR

IT'S VERY CHRISTMASY:

. . . .

Moravian stars, to us, are the classic Christmas decoration!
Making it from cork lets you achieve a special modern look.

MATERIALS

- Per star: 4 strips of cork paper

TOOLS

- Scissors
- Tweezers

NOTE ON THE MATERIALS: SIZING

You can make the Moravian stars in different sizes by adjusting the dimensions of the cork strips. In the following list, you can find the appropriate dimensions specified:

0.4" × 11.8" / 0.6" × 15.7" / 0.8" × 21.3" / 1" × 26.8"

. . . .
HOW IT'S MADE
. . . .

1.

Fold all 4 strips in the middle and then lay them around each other, so as to form a plaited square (Figures 1 and 2).

2.

Now fold the first of the upper strips down. Moving clockwise, fold all the other strips upward (Figure 3).

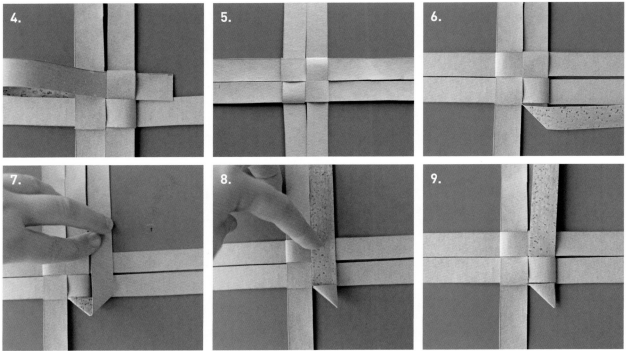

3. The last strip is further drawn through the flap formed by the first folded strip (Figures 4, 5).

4. Take the bottom right strip and fold it to the right, so it lies next to the strip pointing right and creates a small triangle (Figure 6). Fold the same strip upward (Figure 7) and then fold it over to the left. Pull the end of the strip over the triangle, through the flap (Figure 9).

5. Repeat this step 3 times (Figure 10). It's easiest if you keep turning the figure 90 degrees counter-clockwise. Then, the flap on the last strip should be hidden under the strips already used.

6. When the first 4 spikes are finished, turn the star over, and fold 4 spikes on the back side (Figure 11).

7. Finally, form the upright spikes by first laying all the strips in the opposite direction and making sure that they are not on top of each other. All the strips should be coming out from the middle.

8. Fold the strip inward so that it forms a small triangle (Figure 12) and then lift it. The triangle should stand now at a 90-degree angle to the ground (Figure 13).

9. Push the strips under the adjacent flap (for positioning, see Figure 14). It's easiest if you raise the tip of the strip at somewhat of a slant (see in Figure 15 where it shows the strip already through the flap). The tip comes out from the corresponding spike.

10. Repeat this step 3 times, in order to complete the first side of the Moravian star (In Figures 16 and 17, you can see how the last spike emerges).

11. Then, turn the star over and repeat the process on the back side.

12. Finally, shorten the leftover pieces of the strips, the ones that peek out from the spikes. Mind when doing so that you do not cut into the spikes. Should that happen, you can fix the star with some glue (Photo 18).

ATMOSPHERIC TABLE LAMP

The warm cork color lends itself excellently for beautifying lamps or for making lampshades. The cork paper glows in warm brown-red tones and its small patterns transform into pretty shadows on the wall.

MATERIALS

- Cork paper (approx. A3-size, but based on the lamp's circumference)
- Paper
- Round table lamp

TOOLS

- Scissors
- Cutter knife
- Glue
- Ruler
- Pencil
- Cutting mat/surface

HOW IT'S MADE

Tip

- Experiment with alternative shapes or patterns for the lamp on a piece of paper.

1. Measure the circumference and height of your lamp and cut out a corresponding piece of the cork paper. The piece of paper should be 1.6" wider due to the adhesive surface.

2. Now, make a stencil for the pattern. Draw a 0.4" thick line in an S-shape on a sheet of paper. Leave a 0.4" margin on the top and bottom. Lastly, cut out this line so you have a stencil.

3. Draw, with the help of the stencil, a uniform pattern on the back of the cork paper. Make sure that you maintain a gap of about 0.4" at the top and bottom and leave at each page end 0.8" of space for the adhesive surfaces.

4. Score the S-shapes carefully out from the cork paper. Use the cutter knife for this and don't forget the cutting surface.

5. Set the finished cover on the lamp and glue the paper tightly together, so it stays around the lamp.

6. If needed, cut a small opening for the power cable in the paper.

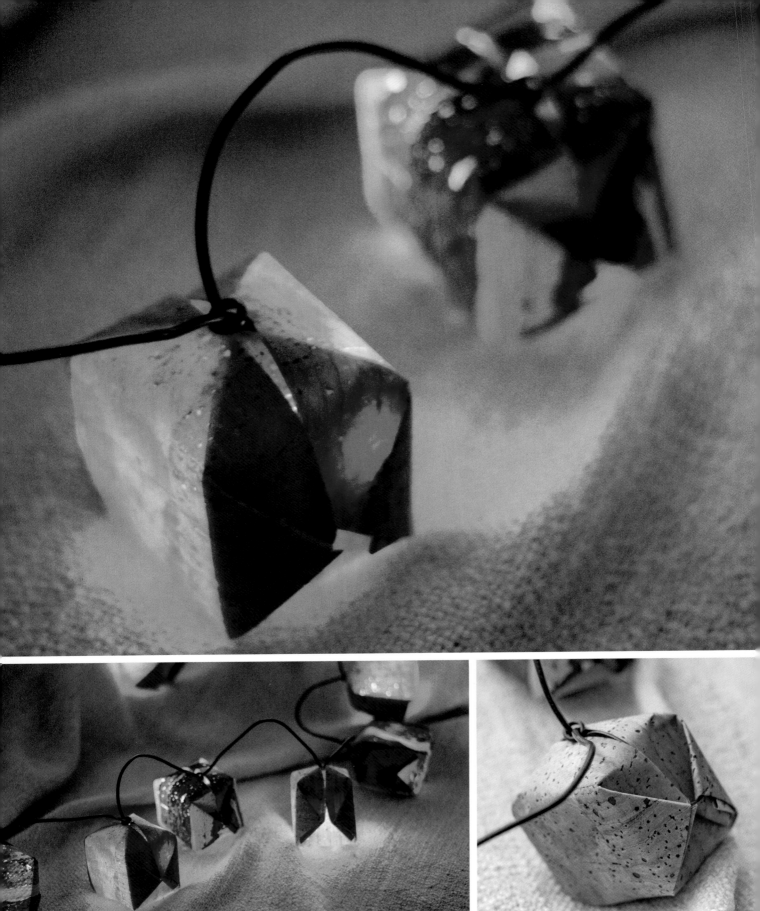

ORIGAMI CUBE LIGHT CHAIN

CORK PAPER HAS A BEAUTIFUL COMPOSITION!

Illuminated, the composition comes into its own beauty! Our origami cube light chain conjures up warm, lovely light.

MATERIALS

- Chain of LED lights, 10 lights
- 10 sheets of cork paper, 7.9" × 7.9"
- Paper towels
- Neutral cooking oil

TOOLS

- Paintbrush
- Ruler
- Scissors

ATTENTION!

As with any chain of lights with paper, make sure that you use LEDs, which do not generate any heat, and that you only use your light chain when you are present.

HOW IT'S MADE

PREPARATION

1. First prepare the cork paper and cut 10 squares of 7.9" × 7.9" paper in the colors of your choice.

2. Coat every corner of the squares on both sides with a thin layer of oil. Check the back of the paper to make sure it is soaked evenly. Lay the squares to dry on highly absorbent paper towels. Cover them with another layer of paper towels and press briefly to absorb the excess oil.

3. Let the paper dry for about 4 hours and then wipe away the last remnants of oil with paper towels. If the paper still feels very greasy to the touch, lay it anew on paper towels and let it dry further.

FOLDING CUBES

1.

Lay the square out in front of you with the cork side facing down.

2.

Fold it once diagonally and run a ruler over the crease to reinforce it. Then, lay the bottom edge onto the top edge and fold the square in the middle. Repeat this step, laying the right edge onto the left edge as you go (Figures 1 and 2).

3.

Take the top edge and lay it on the bottom one. Lightly press the sides inward, so it forms a triangle (Figure 3).

4.

Now, take the bottom right corner of the triangle and lay it on the triangle's tip. Drag the ruler over the fold again and repeat this step for the other 3 corners (Figure 4).

5.

You should now have a diamond shape, as seen in Figure 5.

6.

Take the outer right point and fold it into the middle. Repeat this step anew with the left outer point (Figure 6).

7.

Turn the diamond over and repeat step 6 with the outer points on the back. Then, your folded cube will look just like Figure 7.

8.

Now, fold the lower right point outward, creating the small triangle as seen in Figure 8.

9.

Fold this protruding triangle inward.

10.

Push the resulting triangle through the flap above which it lies. Repeat this step for all 3 lower points (Figures 9 and 10).

11.

Now, inflate the cube by blowing powerfully into the top point and supporting the process by carefully pulling the corners apart. You many need to widen the opening into which you just blew so you can push the LED light through it.

CHRISTMAS STAR LANTERN

It is so very cuddly and cozy in autumn and winter by the candlelight.
Our Christmas Star Lanterns are not so complicated to fold as may
seem upon first glance.

It is worth it, because they spread a beautiful, gentle light!

MATERIALS

- Square cork paper (see selection of sizes)
- Neutral cooking oil
- Paper towels
- Glass and candle (preferably an LED light)

TOOLS

- Paintbrush
- Scissors
- Ruler

ATTENTION!

If you're working with oiled paper, use a glass for the candle because of the increased flammability, or use LED lights.

SELECTION OF SIZES

For this project, you should work with squares with a minimum edge length of at least 9.8". Depending on how far you push the bottom, you'll end up with a lantern approx. 2.8" high and with a maximum diameter of about 4.7". We worked with a 13.8" edge length (3.5" tall, 6.3" in diameter) or 15.7" (4.3" tall, 7.9" in diameter).

TIP FOR FOLDING

Cork can be somewhat more difficult than normal paper to fold so it is very important that you bend all the folding lines at least once in the other direction and firmly smooth with a ruler. Mind that you always fold point-to-point or edge-to-edge.

If you want to practice this technique, you can first fold a normal piece of paper. Cork paper is sometimes a bit unruly so the paper model can help you understand in which direction you must push.

PAPER OILS

Oil your lantern first so that a particularly beautiful light can shine through. First cut out your square and paint a thin layer of neutral cooking oil on both sides. Let it set for a few minutes and then dab the square with some paper towels. Lay it out to dry for another couple of hours between 2 pressed layers of paper towels. Then, rub the paper once again with the paper towels to remove any lasting residue.

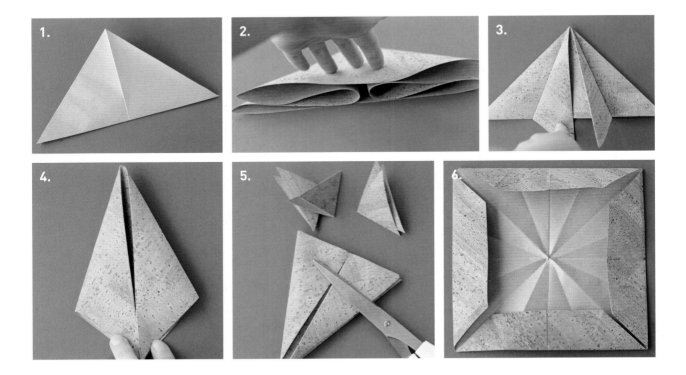

FOLDING THE LANTERNS

The best way to fold is on a paper base or wipeable surface in order to avoid oil stains.

1. Start by folding both of the square's diagonals. Fold each crease at least one time in the other direction and do the same for every other crease in these instructions (Figure 1).

2. Take the square's top edge and bring it to the bottom edge. In doing so, press the sideways triangle inward. You should now have a large triangle (Figure 2).

3. Lay the triangle down with the long side facing you. Fold the upper outer edge into the middle (Figure 3). Turn the figure around and fold the remaining 2 outer edges into the middle.

4. You should now have a small kite (Figure 4). Cut straight out the smaller of the kite's triangles (Figure 5).

5. Unfold everything again to create an octagon. In the middle of each edge there should be the end of a crease line. At 2 opposite points, if the crease is not good or visible at all, fold the paper there again. There should be a total of 16 creases in the paper, which meet in the middle.

6. Now fold the top, bottom, left, and right edges. Align them with existing crease edges, so they are folded about halfway to the middle (Figure 6).

7. Open the fold again and repeat this step with the remaining 4 octagon edges.

8. Now, lay the paper in front of you with the cork side facing down. You should now spot a small kite coming out from the middle, with the short side toward the edge. Fold the in-between pieces between the diamonds inward (Figure 7) and, in doing so, fold the diamonds on top of each other like an accordion (Figure 8).

9. Finally, you must just press the last middle piece inward. You should now have a kite with many pleats on the left side and 1 pleat on the right side (Figure 9).

10. Fold the first point downward (Figure 10) and then fold the long-left edge to the right (Figure 11). Repeat this step until the end, then turn the diamond around and fold the last point.

11. After that, very carefully pull apart your lantern. Press the bottom with your hand, so that your glass can stand inside.

CREATIVE CRAFT IDEAS

MADE FROM CORK CONSTRUCTION PAPER

STAR TABLE DECORATIONS

Cork is a great material for making table decorations to give a dinner a festive touch. 3-D stars are well-suited to folding easily and also just look great in other decorative arrangements!

MATERIALS

- Cork construction paper (see note)

TOOLS

- Circle cutter (alternatively: compasses and scissors)
- Ruler
- Cutter knife
- Glue

NOTE ON THE MATERIALS

For 1 star, you need 2 circles made of cork construction paper. We worked with 6.3" circles, on average, for the large stars and 3.9" circles for the small stars, but you can choose the sizes freely.

Tip

Combine the cork stars with a few other stars made of black construction paper.

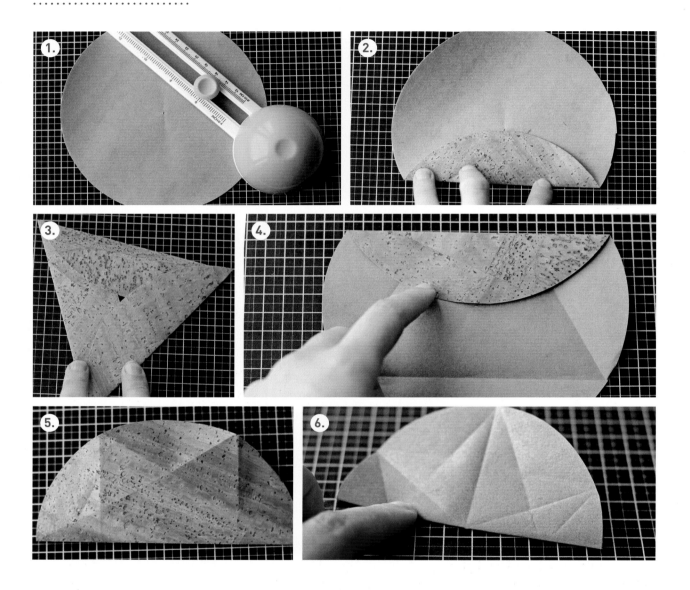

1. Using the circle and circle cutter or the compass and scissors, cut out 2 circles made of cork paper. It's important that you mark the circle's center point.

2. Lay the paper out in front of you with the cork side facing down. Now, fold the circle inward so it touches exactly in the center. Don't fold the paper so it's completely tight, rather run your finger firmly over both edge pieces, and let the middle bend loosely.

3. Fold the other 2 sides, forming a triangle.

4. Now, open the folded parts again. The 3 resulting points should be in the middle. Fold the edges firmly, not the middle portion.

5. There should now be a recognizable 6-pointed star shape on the circle. Fold the circle in half, so the crease runs through the opposite star point. Repeat this twice more with the other star points.

6. Then, turn the paper over so the cork side is on top. Now, fold the paper 3 more times in the middle. This time, the creases should run through the corners of the star.

7. Then, turn the paper again and, using a cutter knife, cut out a piece of the middle portion between the points as seen in photo.

8. Now, cut a small slit in the corner of the star. Do this for all your middle portions and fold them in afterward.

9. When you are finished with the second star, you can dab the resulting flaps with glue and glue the stars together. Run the ruler once more firmly over the long crease through the star's points, if needed.

10. Let the glue dry well and press the star carefully into shape.

Tip

You can also make your own
mobile hanger by buying a
round wire at the hardware
store and binding it tightly.
A round cooling rack can
also work.

LEAVES MOBILE

THE 3-D LEAVES MOBILE GOES WELL IN ROOMS WITH A LOT OF NATURAL LIGHT OR IN FRONT OF A WINDOW.

The cork's texture means the leaves almost look real. Colored cork also works nicely and would go well, for example, in a kid's room.

MATERIALS

- Cork construction paper (approx. 3 A-4 sized sheets)
- Thin thread
- Mobile hanger
- Stencil

TOOLS

- Scissors
- Pen
- Sewing needle

HOW IT'S MADE

1. Print and cut out a leaf stencil or other stencil of your choice.

2. Transfer your stencils onto the construction paper or just draw the leaf or other shapes on it yourself. Cut at least 3 pieces in each leaf or other shape.

3. Prick a hole in the top of the leaves using the needle and thread the thread through.

4. Now, you can hang the leaves. If using a round mobile hanger consisting of an inner ring and an outer ring, use the longest threads for the inner leaves and the shortest threads for the leaves on the outer ring.

CORK-STRIP BASKETS

Small storage baskets are super convenient and allow for order as well. Use different colors of cork paper to weave pretty patterns.

MATERIALS

- Cork paper strips
  (at least 15)

TOOLS

- Glue
- Scissors
- Paper clips

NOTE ON THE SIZE AND LENGTH OF THE STRIPS

You can make the basket in any size. For a small everyday basket, we use strips 0.5" wide and 13.8" long. The finished basket is then approximately 2.8" × 2.8" × 2.8", if you work with 5 strips and match it to the basket in the photo with the cotton swabs.

HOW IT'S MADE

1. Cut out 15 strips 0.5" wide and at least 13.8" long.

2. Lay 5 strips in front of you on a smooth surface and arrange them vertically next to each other. Lay 5 more strips out in preparation. Now, take the first strip and weave it horizontally through the 5 strips, always switching between going over one strip and under the next as you push it through.

3. Weave the second strip directly below the first, beginning in reverse this time. Do this for all 5 strips.

4. You should now see a woven square in front of you. Shift it so that the ends of the strips on all 4 edges are exactly the same length.

5. Now, fold all the protruding strips upward at a 90-degree angle. You can now continue weaving the basket upward. Take a strip and weave it once completely through all protruding strips on all 4 edges. It's best to begin doing so in the middle of one side.

6. Then, weave the next row. For the small basket, we worked a total of 5 strips. Shorten the ends, stick them inward under the plaiting, and fix in place with some glue.

Tip

So that everything adheres well, you can fix the ends with paper clips when drying.

Tip

You can also make the tags out of cork fabric and hang them on a bag. Cork fabric is somewhat more robust than construction paper.

GIFT TAGS

Lovingly wrapped gifts let hearts beat just a bit faster. In only 5 minutes, you can make a small, pretty gift tag that puts the finishing touches on any gift.

MATERIALS

- Cork construction paper
- Ribbon
- Stencil

TOOLS

- Scissors
- Black permanent marker
- Hole punch

MATERIAL SPECS

Per gift tag, approximately 2" × 3.5" on A4 paper

HOW IT'S MADE

1. Draw the different tag shapes on the cork construction paper and cut them out.

2. Make a hole at the top of the tag.

3. Now, you can decorate the tag and write a name on it.

4. Lastly, thread the ribbon through the hole and hang it on the gift.

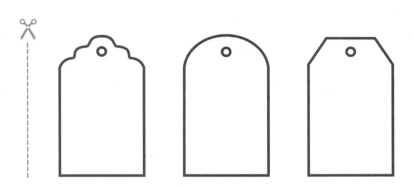

GEO VASES

Fold yourself a unique designer vase made with cork construction paper in just 10 minutes. A drinking glass or a pickle jar from your scrap glass collection doubles quite easily as a vase. The cork paper forms a casing for the glass. To create variety, combine a square vase with a pair of round ones.

MATERIALS

- Cork construction paper
- Drinking glass or scrap glass

TOOLS

- Ruler
- Scissors
- Glue
- Paper clips

MATERIAL SPECS

Custom sizing, depending on the glass. Shown in the example: approximately 11.8" × 5.5"

HOW IT'S MADE

THE BASE

Measure the height and circumference of the glasses and cut out a correspondingly large piece of cork paper. It should be 0.8" wider than the glass in order for the adhesive surface to hold.

ROUND VASE

Glue the 2 ends together, creating the round covering for the vase. Make sure when gluing that the case is not too tight around the vase, so that you can also can remove it.

HEXAGONAL VASE

For hexagonal vases, divide the construction paper beforehand into 6 equally sized pieces. Mark the bending points and then fold firmly inward, using a ruler or another hard object. Lastly, glue them together, like with the round vase.

Tip

Mix several vases with different heights and cork patterns together to create an exciting and decorative vase arrangement.

Translation Copyright © 2019 by Skyhorse Publishing

The original German edition was published as *Feng an mit Kork*

Copyright © 2015 Landwirtschaftsverlag GmbH, 48 165 Münster, Germany (www.lv-buch.de)

This edition is published by arrangement with Claudia Bohme Rights & Literary Agency, Hannover, Germany (www.agency-boehme.com).

Skyhorse Publishing books may be purchased in bulk at special discounts for sales promotion, corporate gifts, fund-raising, or educational purposes. Special editions can also be created to specifications. For details, contact the Special Sales Department, Skyhorse Publishing, 307 West 36th Street, 11th Floor, New York, NY 10018 or info@skyhorsepublishing.com.

Skyhorse® and Skyhorse Publishing® are registered trademarks of Skyhorse Publishing, Inc.®, a Delaware corporation.

Visit our website at www.skyhorsepublishing.com.

10 9 8 7 6 5 4 3 2 1

Library of Congress Cataloging-in-Publication Data is available on file.

Photos: Jutta Handrup, Maike Hedder, Münster; except for Pg. 6, Anastasia Esau, Hannover

Layout & Design: Nina Eckes, www.nina-eckes.de

Print ISBN: 978-1-5107-4024-2
Ebook ISBN: 978-1-5107-4025-9

Printed in China